CW00746170

100% of the proceeds from the sale of Lockdown Letterboxes will be donated to the UK-based charity YoungMinds via Work for Good. YoungMinds is leading the movement to make sure every young person gets the mental health support they need, when they need it, no matter what.

Copyright © 2021 Belinda Goldsmith
All rights reserved.

Collection time
2020 to
2021

A collection of Letterbox
toppers from across
the UK

The Team

Belinda Goldsmith – Author

Belinda trained as a journalist in London and worked for Reuters for 27 years as a foreign correspondent and editor-in-chief of the company's corporate charity, the Thomson Reuters Foundation. She lives in Pinner, NW London. She joined Save the Children's global media team in 2021. She can't knit or crochet but is a dab hand with glitter.

Rose Cussen – Photographer

Rose worked in television for 25 years, directing and promoting on-air campaigns for Sky Sports. She now teaches filmmaking to Masters students at Goldsmiths, University of London, and runs her own photography business from Harrow, NW London. She can't wield a needle but has a sharp eye for a good story.

Pia Smeaton – Designer

Pia was born in the North of England and started her career in London before moving to Australia where she works as a designer in Sydney. With an appreciation for the handmade, she is an obsessive forager of charity shops and markets, seeking the beautiful homemade crochet blankets that are becoming so rare.

Keren Haynes – Publicist

Keren worked as a radio and television journalist in Britain, Dubai and Hong Kong, before shifting gear and moving into communications. She specialises in broadcast and co-owns London-based PR agency Shout! Communications. She lives in Ealing, West London. She expresses her creativity in her garden, taking great pride in her greenhouse.

Contents

01.
Introduction

A funny thing happened during the coronavirus lockdowns in Britain. Brightly coloured knitted or crocheted covers, adorned with flowers, animals, rainbows, nurses, and even the Queen started to appear on the top of letterboxes around the country. Many of these graffiti hats arrived on postboxes overnight and no one knew who had put them up. Some were the work of groups and other by so-called solo bombers. All of them attracted attention.

I first spotted a vivid green cover festooned with flowers on top of a letterbox during one of my morning runs as, like millions of others, I was no longer commuting to work and was battling the bulge sitting at my kitchen desk. I laughed out loud when I first spotted this extraordinary work of art as it was such a funny - but rather lovely – sight. Who had spent the hours to create this well-crafted and intricate scene? I was so amazed that I stopped and took a photo that I put on Instagram. The reaction was even more surprising. "Oh I've seen lots of those," said one friend in Beaconsfield, Buckinghamshire. Another from Devon said she had also spotted these intricate toppers on letterboxes near her. A friend from Nottingham was also non-plussed as these were so common in her neck of the woods.

> *Who had spent the hours to create this well-crafted and intricate scene?*

As a journalist for decades, this piqued my interest. When had graffiti knitting started to hit our streets' iconic red letterboxes? Who were the people behind this emerging movement of guerrilla knitters and crocheters that had spread nationwide while I was busy watching "Normal People" and "I May Destroy You" and gesticulating "you're on mute" to colleagues on video calls? But also how had their lives changed during lockdown. This was a topic worth exploring as I realised that letterbox toppers were not only the handiwork of the elderly – no offence meant! From the young to the old, from students to retirees, to those shielding to frontline workers, the range of people making these covers was extraordinary and provided a unique view on how the entire country was adapting to the loss of freedom in the face of a global pandemic. There was also the added edge that some were made anonymously – and no one knew if they were actually allowed to put graffiti art on postboxes.

I enlisted the help of several friends - Rose, a photographer, Pia, a graphic designer, and Keren, a communications expert - and set out to uncover the story of Lockdown Letterboxes.

The covers were cute and funny – but also very British, very lovely, and very quirky. They became a symbol of lockdown as we all had to find new ways to Keep Calm and Carry On, spending more time than ever at home, with our families, on Zoom calls, and in our local communities as walking or running became our main sources of exercise.

Across the UK, we spoke to dozens of graffiti knitters and crocheters – some of whom remain anonymous - about why they got involved, the reaction they received, but also how they and their families had coped with this unprecedented time in British history. We had been told that this was going to be the biggest challenge for the world since World War Two, with millions of deaths and the likelihood of a recession with no parallel in the recent past. The loss of loved ones, job redundancies, the surge in mental health problems and overall worries about the future had put the country on edge and everyone reacted differently. To me it made sense to record this moment, this snapshot in time, when, faced with a global pandemic of terrifying proportions, some Brits took up their knitting needles and crochet hooks to keep busy, brighten up neighbourhoods, and raise money for charity.

we drafted a list of 50 moments, trends and people that impacted our lives and homes.

In Lockdown Letterboxes we take a look at the origins of yarn bombing and track down the history of postbox toppers in Britain. We present the stories of 16 people, aged 17 to 80, from London to Leeds, from the Home Counties to the Highlands, from the west coast to Wales, who joined this growing army of graffiti knitters during lockdown. We opted to present 16 stories to represent the 16 months from when the first lockdown started in March 2020 to when social distancing was scheduled to end in June 2021. We make no judgment on how Britain handled the pandemic but we do give you a timeline, illustrated by seasonal toppers of key facts during those 16 months.

We realised we were all starting to forget some of the key events of lockdown so, with the collaboration of numerous friends and family members, we drafted a list of 50 moments, trends and people that impacted our lives and homes. Finally we tried to show exactly how far and wide this craze had spread, but once we had uncovered more than 100 places across the country with letterbox toppers we stopped counting. I am sure there are even more towns and villages that joined this craze so do share any you have spotted with the Lockdown Letterboxes accounts on Instagram, Facebook and Twitter. We hope you enjoy the book as much as we all enjoyed researching and producing it as we tried to focus on something positive after such a dreadful year. All proceeds from sales go to YoungMinds, a UK charity which works to promote the mental health of children whose lives were turned upside down by this pandemic.

02.
How It Began

Time after time, the people I spoke to who were creating these letterbox artworks stressed that this was nothing new, as yarn bombing, yarn storming, guerrilla knitting, or graffiti knitting – whatever you want to call it – had been around for some time.

With this new type of street art, graffiti knitters and crocheters wrapped their works around trees, lamp posts, monuments, benches, and all kinds of static parts of the cityscape.

The history of yarn bombing is a bit vague but the edgy, street version is widely believed to have really kicked-off in Houston, Texas, in the United States and is attributed to Magda Sayeg who is proud to be called the Queen of Yarnbombing. After all she coined the term when she covered the door handles of her boutique with hand-made pink and purple knitted cosies back in 2005.

When this small act attracted the attention of passers-by, Magda realised she was onto something and started to experiment with enhancing the ordinary, the functional, the boring, the ugly, with tailored knitted suits. She started first with small "yarn bombs" such as sign poles and fire hydrants in her hometown, and then ventured further into urban landscapes, even covering a bus one time, along the way establishing the yarn bombing crew, Knitta Please.

Knitta, as it was known, grew to 11 members by the end of 2007, with the members - just like any street graffiti gang – staying anonymous and donning monikers such as AKrylik and PolyCotN. Magda went under the name Knitta and other members included Knotorious N.I.T., SonOfaStitch (my favourite!) and P-Knitty. The group would tag their work with slogans like "knitta please" and "whaddup knitta?".

Photo: Magda Sayeg

The group didn't last long but by then, however, the idea had hooked others – with various other groups setting up in the United States and other countries.

I managed to track Magda down to Brooklyn in New York where she is now running a restaurant called Magdalene – a Lebanese American eatery to commemorate her father's heritage. Magda, now 47, said she had no idea on that rainy day when she wrapped those door handles in knitted covers that it would change her life.

"I never in my wildest dreams thought that putting that cosy on that door handle would change my entire life but it did," she told me. "But I was ready to dream big with it. I wanted to nurture it".

The reaction she got from people spurred her on, and she became addicted to bringing inanimate objects to life. For her it was more than just a fun thing to do. It was making a statement in our fast-paced life as yarn bombing made people stop and look twice.

"Seeing the reaction to the cosy I realised the urban environment was my playground and I went from there. This was just as the World Wide Web was starting up and it picked up immediately. Local and national media got interested and it took off," she said.

"There was a lot of growing pains as I had no idea what I was walking into. I was a single mother with three children and I didn't fit the profile of someone who is an artist or someone who can be taken seriously in art globally."

Magda no longer associates as a yarn bomber but she has gone on to give talks about her life, including to students setting out on careers. I asked her what message she wanted to get across.

"I thought it was really important to tell people that life is a not always going to be A to B, with school, college, a career. My life has been all over the place and I needed more satisfaction than that. I tell people life can be A to C. You never know what is going to pop up but don't take a back seat.

"Yarn bombing is great for taking a risk. With yarn bombing you are empowering your own environment and making something happen without permission. That is very powerful. It is technically illegal but that can be a thrill too."

Had she seen the postbox toppers in Britain?

"Someone mentioned them to me and what a great thing to do! What a nice gesture to communicate to others at this time and say we are still here. That is a beautiful message to people in the time of COVID and that is why I love public art events.

"For me yarnbombing was a wild ride and I held on tight and fought for it. I am proud to say that I am a working artist today."

And art it now is, with museums and galleries around the world hosting yarn bombing exhibitions including the Museum of Arts and Design in New York, London's Hayward Gallery, and Munich's Deutsches Museum. Several books have been written about yarn bombing.

There's even International Yarn Bombing Day – June 11 – which was started by Joann Matvichuk of Lethbridge in the Canadian province of Alberta. It is a day when some communities allow knitted and crochet artworks to be hung on trees and signs, around lamp posts and woven through bike racks.

But while yarn bombing may have gone mainstream, for some this practice is still seen as an act of subversion, sometimes as a feminist statement. For after all it is taking crafts such as knitting, crochet, sewing and embroidery - traditionally mainly reserved for women and identified with domesticity - into a hipper space. What adds to the attraction is that the peaceful aspect of these crafts can attract a far wider and diverse demographic than marching in street protests or waving placards. Grandmas are happy to wield their needles alongside teenagers in these projects.

International Yarn Bombing Day – June 11

The ethics of yarn bombing, however, does still make some crafters uneasy. Some boroughs frown upon residents wrapping street signs in wool. Environmentalists have been vocal about the harm this can do to trees, stifling their growth if wrapped around trunks and branches, and also concerned about the damage to wildlife if yarn is left out to rot. Others think the yarn could be put to better use, such as making clothing for the needy.

I tracked down Lauren O'Farrell, the founder of London-based Knit the City, one of the UK's most notorious yarn bombing collectives, to ask for her views on yarn bombing and how she got involved. Lauren, from Crystal Palace in southeast London, who also goes by the moniker Deadly Knitshade, created the Stitch London craft community and has written three books on knitting including "Knit the City: A Whodunnknit Set in London" that was published in 2011.

"When I started back in 2007 or so I had no idea of the power of yarn bombing," she told me.

"I first started as I was going through treatment for Hodgkin Lymphoma. I was in hospital on-and-off for three years. While I was there I couldn't read or write as chemotherapy makes your brain fluffy and I needed something else to keep me busy. I got my mum to teach me how to knit thinking it would be a nice easy thing to learn. It was not that easy. I have still never knitted a garment. But I found it very productive and creative.

"When I got better I decided to use knitting to make a bit of a statement about the fact that I was still alive. While I had been ill I could not really take public transport and I ended up walking a lot and seeing a lot of street art and it was a community I really wanted to be part of.

"I wanted to put characters on my work and use it to tell stories and history. I didn't want it to stay forever or to get anyone cross.

"Yarn bombing and all kinds of temporary artwork should be a bit like when you are walking alone at night and you see a fox in the road. He looks at you and you look at him and for a moment it is special. Then it has gone. It shouldn't last forever although the images can last for ages."

Over the years creative crafters in numerous towns have joined forces to yarn bomb their high streets and city centres for certain festivals. From Bognor on the south coast to Wrexham in Wales, from Tring in Hertfordshire to Great Malvern in Worcestershire, benches, fences and bollards, have ended up covered in wool to brighten up the town.

Olivia Dieterich, who lives in Loughborough but was raised in Wolverhampton, said yarn bombing had helped to drive a revival of crochet and knitting in recent years which is why she set up the group Random Acts of Crochet Kindness in 2019. She was amazed by the interest with the group's Facebook page which now has more than 30,000 members.

"I set the group up because I was fed up with the stigma that only grannies could crochet and if you were young and crocheted then you weren't cool," she said — and Olivia should know. She is 24.

"We've tried to change that and get more young people involved at a time when you can see interest is growing, with crochet tops back in fashion. But I was surprised to see how many people joined our group. And when lockdown started even more people joined."

As lockdown began, members of Random Acts of Crochet Kindness were mainly making little trinkets, like flowers and hearts, and leaving them anonymously in public places with notes attached, telling the finders to take them home if they liked them. It was about spreading kindness.

"Initially there was a lot of anxiety about leaving trinkets for people to find and concern about whether people would get in trouble for leaving things in a public place during a pandemic. So people started to get creative, thinking of other things that cannot be removed or taken home - and letterbox toppers just exploded.

"It seemed to come from nowhere and all of sudden everyone was doing it. It has just been a massive thing. It is amazing how people have found different ways to adapt at this time. For a lot of people this has been the thing that has kept them going and given them a sense of purpose."

yarn bombing had helped to drive a revival of crochet and knitting in recent years

I asked Lauren for her views on the latest lockdown form of yarn bombing – letterbox toppers.

"During lockdown you have so many people who have suddenly had the entertainment they normally have taken away from them. There are no cafés, no theatres. Hobbies like jigsaws have gone wild," she said.

"I really think graffiti knitting in particular has struck a chord with people in that it is fairly easy and you don't have to put a massive effort into it. A lot of people are finding their voices while they are stuck indoors and seeing people trying to save their sanity like this has been quite glorious."

03.
Letterbox Craze

So when exactly did these knitted hats start to appear on the top of letterboxes in Britain? We know the numbers have skyrocketed during lockdown but no one seemed to know when the first person decided to knit a cosy for a postbox. I set myself the task of tracking this down.

Quite a few people mentioned Herne Bay in Kent to me and I came across press clippings about the Herne Bay Cosy Club which started making toppers for Christmas 2015. Bingo – or so I thought! For as I read through the comments on their social media posts I noticed one person mentioning that they had seen postbox toppers before, in Southend-on-Sea. I tracked down Sara Worley, who started the Cosy Club, and she confirmed that she got the idea from a now-disbanded group in Southend called The Craft Club Yarnbombers.

Next step? To find members of that group. Back to Google and I dug up a BBC article from 2014 that featured a group of five teachers from Southend who set up The Craft Club Yarnbombers and were making postbox toppers. The article even mentioned the school where they worked. I called to try to find that gang of five – but unfortunately they had all left and, with GDPR on data protection and privacy, I hit

Photos: Gabby Atkins Southend-on-Sea

another dead end. The school was not nearly as enthused as I was about the possibility that this group could have made history as the first in Britain to cover a postbox with graffiti knits.

Royal Mail couldn't help me on the history hunt. I tried two of the country's leading knitting and crochet magazines. They didn't know. I asked knitters and crocheters galore. They didn't know. I even asked Southend-on-Sea Borough Council.

"We would be delighted if it was the case that Southend started this trend but we have been unable to confirm that," council spokesman Tony Smyth told me.

I was about to give up when one of the numerous messages I sent over social media finally paid off. Gabby Atkins, one of the five teachers to set up The Craft Club, messaged me back – and confirmed that Southend-on-Sea was the pioneer of postbox graffiti toppers in Britain in 2014.

"Yarn bombing was massive in America and we were looking for something that would attract an audience and was community based. So we decided to put something on top of a postbox on the seafront where there is a lot of foot traffic so lots of people would see it. Our first topper had a seagull on it and then we did a snow one for Christmas that year," Gabby told me by phone.

"We then started to drive around to look for other postboxes that would be good to yarn bomb with the aim being to give something to the community and get people engaged. We hadn't seen anyone else do this so I do think postbox toppers probably were our idea.

"We did ask Royal Mail and were told that as long

as we didn't block the door or prevent people from putting mail in the box then it was OK," said Gabby, explaining that the group disbanded in 2019 as their career paths went in different directions.

Mystery solved. From 2015 onwards, this new form of graffiti street art started to slowly gather pace, with toppers popping up at Christmas in a few towns around the country.

The Secret Society of Hertford Crafters put their first toppers up in 2017, getting the idea after one member spotted the woolly covers in Herne Bay, said organiser Jo Baily. Twenty friends got together - and Hertford had its own toppers. The publicity was contagious.

Clare Suttie, from nearby St Albans also in Hertfordshire, said she was inspired to start yarn bombing postboxes after meeting someone from the Hertford Crafters and hearing how much they raised for a local hospice. Before you could say knit one purl one, Clare and her friend Candy Stuart were trudging the streets in the lead up to Christmas installing 23 postbox toppers. They raised £4,000 for charity. The next year the group, St Albans Postboxes, installed 50 toppers in St Albans, Wheathampstead, Harpenden, Redbourn and Hemel Hempstead, and raised more than £12,000.

When lockdown hit, the now enthused group created 12 flower-themed toppers plotted out on a map at a time when a walk was the highlight of the day for many. The money raised went to the St Albans and District Food Bank run by The Trussell Trust and a local charity for the homeless, Open Door. Clare said by this time the toppers were well known locally and the response at Christmas 2020 – nine months after the start of the first lockdown – was incredible with more than £27,000 raised for the two nominated charities easily. Each topper was sponsored by a local business and had a QR code attached so people could donate to the nominated charities with a swipe or two on their smartphone.

"This jump in what we raised was due to a combination of that usual feeling of goodwill at Christmas but also this was the year when people who could donate felt a strong urge to do so. We had a lot of larger donations, like £100 from families, which we normally wouldn't expect. We were astonished,"said Clare.

The craze was spreading – and what's more, Royal Mail didn't seem to mind.

Royal Mail has about 115,000 pillar, wall, and lamp boxes across Britain. A small number are listed buildings as some postboxes are deemed to make a significant contribution to an area. So much so that in 2002, English Heritage (now Historic England) and Royal Mail, with the approval of the Department for Culture, Media and Sport (DCMS), agreed a joint policy for the retention and conservation of all Royal Mail postboxes.

Bit of a step back in time here for history buffs – and I have taken this account from Royal

Mail as there were numerous accounts. It was Post Office official-turned-novelist Anthony Trollope – best known for his series of novels collectively known as the "Chronicles of Barsetshire" – who introduced the pillar box to Britain in 1852 when he was working in Jersey in the Channel Islands. He adopted a system used on the Continent of putting locked cast-iron pillar boxes at the roadside with regular collection times.

His scheme was extended to the mainland in 1853. Some of the first postboxes were hexagonal in shape but designs varied. However in 1859 a standard cylindrical design was created for use nationwide with a posting slot under a cap for protection from the weather. Soon came a variety of new designs including the elegant hexagonal box, first seen in 1866, with a cap decorated with acanthus leaves designed by the architect J.W. Penfold.

The Letter Box Study Group, an organisation devoted to the study of postboxes and the recognised authority on the issue, has identified about 800 different types of postbox, including about 400 different varieties of pillar box.

"No other country has the variety of postboxes that we have or the depth of interest," said a trustee of the group, Robert Cole. *"It is a bit trainspotterish but we wear our anoraks with pride."*

It was not until 1874 that postboxes were painted the familiar red and this became the standard colour that can only be varied in exceptional circumstances, with genuine historical reasons. This included when 110 boxes were painted gold in celebration of the London 2012 British Olympic and Paralympic champions. To reflect the iconic nature of the British postbox and the heritage attached to them, out-of-use postboxes - especially older models - are often left in place and painted black and sealed to signify the box is no longer in use.

Ruislip Arts and Crafters

LEGAL OR ILLEGAL?

The long and the short of it is, don't mess with Britain's postboxes. So are you allowed to put covers on postboxes?

Several of the graffiti knitters I spoke to said they had been wary about this. Some had asked their local post office and got nothing but positive feedback and praise for brightening up the street and making people smile. Others didn't ask but just went ahead. One woman – who shall remain nameless – said a man at Royal Mail told her it wasn't really legal but go ahead anyway – and remember that this conversation had never happened.

I asked Royal Mail if people were allowed to install toppers.

"Over the years we have enjoyed seeing the various postbox toppers that different groups have showcased in local communities across the UK. We first began to see these toppers over the festive season, although this soon spread to other key times of the year such as Easter. More recently, we have noticed decorations celebrating various frontline workers during the pandemic, including postal workers," said a spokesperson for Royal Mail.

"Royal Mail's iconic postboxes are a treasured part of communities around the UK and are for use by our customers. For those groups who enjoy crocheting, knitting, and decorating our thousands of postboxes across the country, we generally advise to please ensure that the decoration doesn't cause a safety concern or any kind of offence. Care should also be taken to ensure the toppers do not obstruct other customers from posting items, or our posties from collecting mail. We appreciate the residents' passion for creating these works of art, and value their interest in Royal Mail."

Royal Mail could not tell me how many letterboxes around the country were topped with these woolly scenes created by groups or single crafters known as solo bombers. We stopped counting the locations boasting toppers when we hit 100. Some of those places have, at times, had up to 50 toppers at any one time so it is probably a fair guess to say more than 1,000.

The biggest pockets of postbox toppers are usually the work of groups rather than solo bombers. I do, however, need to give a shout-out here to probably the most prolific topper trouper in Britain, retired policewoman Rachel Williamson from Rhyl in Wales, who made over 70 of varying designs from when lockdown started in March 2020 to June 2021.

More and more craft groups have emerged during lockdown which has also fuelled the craze. Fran Tracey set up the Ruislip Arts and Crafters at the end of 2020 when London was in Tier 4 with a miserable looking winter looming. She thought about 40-50 people would join, but it took off and the numbers surged to about 700 within weeks.

"We were amazed. We initially thought we might start with yarn bombing but the group was divided as there has been issues with putting knitted items around living things such as trees, so then someone else suggested postbox toppers," said Fran.

The group made their first toppers for Valentine's Day, some knitted, some crochet and some fabric. They proved so popular that for spring the group made about 30, largely with Easter and Mother's Day themes, with Fran running some free Google Meet tutorials to teach people how to make the bases and one member of the group drawing up a trail of the postboxes for people to walk around. Summer toppers featuring mermaids were next in the pipeline. One of the most talked about ones was installed outside a local post office with a post van and postman – in a mask.

Fran, 55, who is a freelance writer of women's fiction for magazines, said the initiative had taken off in a way that no one had anticipated.

"We've had a bit of vandalism and theft and that can be quite hard to deal with it as it is such a shame. But you have to adopt a bit of a c'est la vie attitude and try to keep positive about it," she said. *"This has just caused some amazing connections at this time when many people are lonely – connecting not just the members of the group – but also the community."*

Christine Allsopp, organiser of the group Yarn Bomb Hemel Hempstead in Hertfordshire, said the number of people interested in getting involved soared during lockdown. The group's membership numbers went from 200 to 600.

"It has been a lifesaver for some people. Like a lot of people I was on furlough, from a recruitment company, and this has kept me busy. Lots of women have said if they were working still they couldn't do it. It has connected people," she said.

Yarn Bomb Hemel Hempstead

Photo: Wendy Kelly, Edinburgh

Edinburgh Spotlight

MON

Last Collection Time
Monday to Frida
5.00pm
A later collection is made at 7.30pm
from the Postbox at
Abbi Centre
53 Cultins Road, Sighthill
Saturday
12.15pm

"When one goes missing the community gets very uptight about it. We do usually get one stolen, usually near a pub, but we will keep on going. Our more recent display has been of keyworkers and we have 20 toppers for that as we wanted to show our support for them and not just NHS workers – my son is a doctor – but for the ones who are forgotten."

Vandalism and theft are a daily risk for toppers. Several creators we spoke too said they had lost toppers or had to mend ones that had been damaged.

Wendy Kelly, 48, a medical herbalist from Leith in Edinburgh, said she was very nervous when she put up her first topper in February 2020 - a rainbow hat - as she lived in a busy urban area. Having crocheted for years, she spotted the toppers during lockdown and decided to try to cheer up her community. She was finding lockdown hard as she was working from home, trying to home-school her two children, while her husband lost all his work as a musician and was working in a warehouse.

Ickenham Postbox Toppers

"We do get a lot of anti-social behaviour so I knew there was a chance my topper would disappear within hours but I thought it was worth the risk if it made people smile," said Wendy.

"I snuck out on a Wednesday just before midnight with my husband to put up my topper. I can see the postbox from my living room so we kept watch and within about two minutes someone stopped and took a photo.

"The next day I was half expecting my topper not to be there but it was and I could see people stopping and taking photos and laughing and smiling about it. I didn't own up for a couple of days but I did add a note to the topper praising our posties who have been amazing throughout everything.

"Then someone slashed it down the middle and stole the pompom. I sewed it back up and added another pompom and it lasted another seven days but then it *disappeared and never appeared again. But I never thought it would last 10 days. I think thousands of people saw it in that time. I haven't done another one as with pubs opened again I don't think it would last two minutes."*

Some people had toppers go missing to then get reports of their work appearing on a letterbox in a different area.

But one of the more unusual stories was a mass theft in Ickenham in Hillingdon. The newly formed group, Ickenham Postbox Toppers, had managed to pull out all the stops to make 17 toppers to cover all the postboxes in the village in time for Easter, hoping to provide some family entertainment with a postbox trail over the long weekend. But on Easter Saturday morning eight had gone missing. The local neighbourhood watch group jumped into action and, using CCTV and doorbell cameras, managed to identify the vehicle of the culprit. The police were called in and all eight toppers were later recovered from a nearby house.

A spokeswoman from London's Metropolitan Police Service confirmed the police were called on Sunday, April 4, to reports of a theft and the property stolen was "a quantity of letterbox knitted toppers".

"No arrests have been made at this stage. Enquiries are continuing," said the spokeswoman.

This experience made the group wary when they threw all their muscle into creating a topper to put up outside Windsor Castle for the funeral of Prince Philip, the Duke of Edinburgh, on April 17. The topper was the piece de resistance of the group, featuring the Queen, Prince Philip, a Land Rover, the Royal Yacht Britannia, and Duke of Edinburgh awardees. Group founder Jane Ellis installed the topper in Windsor on the eve of the funeral and took it down again at 5pm the next day. In those 24 hours it featured on the front page of the London Evening Standard, in The Times, on the BBC and in newspapers around the world.

"We were worried it was going to be pinched," said Jane Ellis, one of 10 group members who were involved in making the Royal topper.

"But we were amazed at the coverage we got. It was a crazy few days. Now our plan is to tidy it up and send it to the Queen."

I could not find any cases of arrests or charges being laid relating to the theft or vandalism of toppers, so I asked the Crown Prosecution Service about any such action.

Spokesman Robert Cox was a bit thrown by the query initially but went away to do some research to find out how such cases were handled.

"The police investigate crimes and our role is quite limited," he reported back. "We decide if there is enough to put before a jury".

Jane Ellis, Ickenham

TOP SECRET TOPPERS

With these question marks over legality, some graffiti knitters have decided to remain anonymous. Some started off yarn bombing their local postbox under the cover of darkness but then owned up, while others have gone all out to protect their identity.

Sharon Trebilcock, 65, started installing her graffiti art secretly as she was new to Garforth in Leeds and was uncertain what her neighbours would think. However the reaction she received to her toppers – covered in pompoms or with dangling tokens that can be removed and taken home - was so positive that she started to own up.

"At first my husband and I did night-time ninja operations to put up new tokens as I didn't know anyone and people might think I was strange doing this but a neighbour spotted me. I have now met people and know far more people than when I first moved in. It has provoked social interaction, human contact, and joy, at a time when we needed it," she said.

Sharon Trebilcock, Leeds

Andy Killpack, Watford

The Villiers Coffee House in Oxhey Village, Watford, has had three toppers on the postbox outside its front door in the past six months. Each time the topper has been changed overnight with no clues left about the postbox yarn bomber.

"They are a bit of a knitting Banksy. No one has owned up to it although we assume it is someone in the village," said café co-owner Andy Killpack. "We have thought about putting up CCTV but so far it remains a bit of a mystery. We get lots of people taking photos of the postbox. The toppers are lovely and do cheer people up."

But the anonymous topper intriguing even topper creators themselves is the so-called Syston Knitting Bankxy from Leicestershire whose artworks have become the envy of many – especially a WWI soldier surrounded in poppies made for Remembrance Day in November 2020. It was based on a soldier who returned to the town after the war.

I asked the town manager of Syston Town Council, Catherine Voyce, if anyone knew who was behind these amazing artworks. They started out with an Easter letterbox topper in 2019 and included one in April 2021 of all the players of Leicester City FC ahead of their FA Cup Semi-Final against Southampton – which they won 1-0. They went on to win the Cup for the first time ever in May.

"As a council we don't know who is doing it. It could be one person or it could be a group even. We can only contact them through social media and the fact they are anonymous has added to the interest," Catherine said.

"I was amazed at first that they didn't get stolen but everyone really appreciates them. They used to only appear around major festivals but they've become more frequent during lockdown and just seem to get better and better.

Photo: Syston Town News

"As a council we think it is great and we encourage them. They add to the diversity of how you can cheer up your town centre. If it's not doing any damage or any environmental harm then we have no objections."

One person who does know the real identity of the mystery knitter is Fiona Henry, editor of community newspaper, the Syston Town News, who has spoken on behalf of the graffiti artist to local media and on local radio. Fiona, however, was giving nothing away.

"There is a small close-knit group who know who it is and help to get the toppers onto the postbox but we are sworn to secrecy. It would spoil it if it came out as it is a bit like Banksy. They are quite happy being anonymous. It adds to the intrigue," said Fiona, who is working on a 2022 charity calendar featuring works by the Syston Knitting Bankxy.

"During lockdown their work has become even more appreciated by people and postbox toppers really have become a thing everywhere it seems. They bring

Photo: Syston Town News

a smile to people's faces. My worry is that if their identity was revealed then this might not happen again as they don't want it to be about them but about the creations."

I was not to be deterred, however, and I continued to plug away at the magical communications channels of social media – and I found the mystery knitter. In a Facebook Messenger exchange she – or he – told me their only agenda was to make people smile.

"These knitted toppers do seem to bring a lot of joy wherever they crop up and they seem to be quite popular now ... It is possible that knitters have extra time on their hands or perhaps they want to spread a little positivity in what has been a gloomy and uncertain time," said the Syston Bankxy.

"I was particularly proud of my WWI Tommy soldier made for Remembrance. I knew how special it was going to be when I got about half-way through it. I was quite choked up by the time it was completed, and hope that it did what it was meant to ... to help us remember those who made the ultimate sacrifice.

"I feel there is no need for my identity to be public because I don't really want recognition ... I'm happy to stay in the shadows, sneaking around my hometown at 4 a.m.. ... I have enjoyed comments of hope for my identity to remain secret which seems to add a little magic. Having said that, I feel for my dad who wants to shout from the rooftops that his child is the creator of the knitted artwork."

I asked them if they considered yarn bombing to be graffiti.

"I think that it is easy to feel sad when our hometowns are littered or smeared with graffiti. But as one lady commented: 'If this is graffiti, I'm happy to see it'. I'd never thought of it like that, and yes, perhaps it is a form of graffiti, but one which gives joy... and it's easily removed."

And what's the harm in that!

04.
Lives Under Lockdown

LINDA CATLING, 74,

Retired optical area trainer, on shielding

"The reason I got into making toppers was because at the start of the pandemic I lost half my sight. I just woke up and it was gone. I have had no end of brain scans but they can't find the cause and without knowing the cause they can't treat it. The optic nerves were damaged and I have been left partially sighted. I was already shielding due to other health issues. At the start I didn't think I would be able to pick up a knitting needle or a crochet hook again but I really needed something to keep me occupied.

My daughter-in-law suggested I make some teddy bears as people were putting them in their windows for children on a bear hunt. Instead I started making masks for the teddies that I gave to neighbours and I thought I would make a mask for the local postbox which I can see from my window. I realised it was too hard so I thought I would put a hat on the postbox instead to thank the NHS. Then I moved onto an autumn hat and a poppy one for Remembrance Day. I have made a Peaky Blinders hat and a Christmas hat. I started at the beginning of lockdown and I have made 17 toppers in total.

I started to be called Banksy of Leigh. At first no one knew who was putting the toppers on but I went public because I wanted to thank people for all the lovely comments online.

It has started a bit of a trend. There is someone doing them near Southend Hospital. A woman around the corner is also making them. It has been my lifesaver really. I don't go out but I can watch people stop to look at them from my window and people wave as they go past. An 87-year-old woman who had her hip done said it gave her the incentive to walk half a mile to see the postbox. While she was there she started to chat to people.

I now have a white cane and I am officially partially sighted but I have a very good husband who does everything for me. The only thing he doesn't do is knit or crochet. This has been really good for me to give me a sense of achievement, the fact I have managed to make them with my eyesight.

People are intrigued about the next one - and it is going to be controversial. I live on a road with double yellow lines on both sides and the speed limit is 30 mph but people tear down it at 70 mph. Nothing is being done about it. So I am knitting a speed camera and on the topper there will also be two cars upside down, an ambulance, a police car, and a fire engine. I have been shielding for the whole year but looking at these postbox toppers and the reaction of people has given me a lot of enjoyment."

FACT

When lockdown started the government advised **2.2 million** clinically extremely vulnerable people across England to shield, with an extra **1.7 million** added to the list in February 2021.

LINDA CATLING – **Leigh-on-Sea, Essex** PHOTO CREDIT

30

KILL YOUR SPEED AND
KEEP EVERYONE SAFE !!

MARINE PARADE

AMEERA DULLOO, 17,

School student, on GCSE exams

"I started to crochet in about June, three months after the first lockdown started. My school had closed and I really had no work to do in the first six months as at that stage schools didn't know how to use the technology. That probably wasn't great for my brain. But I was told in March - literally the day the schools were closing - that GSCEs had been cancelled.

Lots of my friends were worried as our teachers had told us not worry too much about our mocks as we had expected to get those over and then revise properly. I was actually quite grateful for the lack of stress. In the end I got 10 GCSEs and incredible grades - I got all 9s except for two 8s. Other friends had a lot of uncertainty though and got worried. Some didn't get into the A levels they wanted. Now I don't know how A-levels will go because I haven't had that kind of stress before. I am doing maths, further maths, and physics. Nothing arty at all.

On the first lockdown I was quite productive. I watched 'Gossip Girl', Netflix and we had movie night every night, my two sisters and me. We played more board games, I did a lot of cooking and Joe Wicks every morning with my mum. My sister and I did the Couch to 5K.

My friend knows how to skateboard so we started to learn how to do that. I texted people and FaceTimed people. I spent a lot of time watching TikTok. In the end I deleted the app in about October last year. Tik Tok is so addictive.

Then I took up crochet. I learnt how to crochet from YouTube. I fiddle a lot and my mum said I should do something with my hands. She knits. I made little squares

FACT

In March 2020 the UK government announced that **GCSE and A Level exams were to be cancelled,** an unprecedented action in UK educational history, and grades would be given out based on predicted grades and teacher assessment.

and learnt individual stitches. The first thing I made was a hat. Then a cardigan. Then a friend of my mum's encouraged her in February to join the Ruislip Arts and Crafters club so I could make something for the postboxes. I started off making flowers.

The toppers are so cool. My friends know that I crochet and they send me pictures of different postbox toppers they see. They genuinely brighten your day - and they are for charity. I've tried to convince my friend to also start crocheting. We all really miss school. I was worried about COVID and I didn't leave the house too much. I didn't get bored or lonely as I was with my family.

When this is all over I will stick with crochet and I hope my skills improve. As for running - I'm not good at it. I'm slow and I fell over once so it wasn't the greatest experience. I don't think I will keep that going."

AMEERA DULLOO – **Eastcote, Middx**

JOHN COLE-MORGAN, 43,

Small business owner on closing up shop

"Our group usually makes three postbox toppers a year but as part of yarn bombing of the whole town centre, with our latest display taking a spring theme with a bee on the topper. I took over as chairman of the Tring Yarn Bomb (in Hertfordshire) in 2015 and our first big event was for the Queen's 90th birthday in 2016. The ladies made so many things and we took them up to Buckingham Palace to deliver them. We got a lovely letter back from the Queen. The oldest person involved in that was 94 and the youngest was three so it really is all ages. All of our events are for charity and we've raised more than £3,000 so far. But postbox toppers during lockdown have taken off like no one would have expected. I don't make them but the ladies do an amazing job.

I opened my shop, Beginner's Quilt Emporium, about three years ago but closed as soon as we went into lockdown in March 2020. I didn't want to open again until June 2021 as so many of my customers are 60 or older. I didn't want to put them at risk or be the cause of someone getting ill. Moving online wasn't going to work as you can't buy fabric online. I did a FaceBook Live every day at 1pm to give everyone a laugh and giggle and keep people going. It certainly helped keep me going.

I started quilting about seven years ago when I was going through a mid-life crisis and, rather than buying a sports car, I wanted to be productive. Until then I had been an accountant. I was taught to knit by my grandmother when I was a child in South Africa and had enjoyed it. It is great to find your passion. But lockdown has been terrible for the business. I had to be protective of my customer base though.

Luckily the government has supported small businesses like mine. I have not had to pay rent while the studio was closed. I have stayed really busy throughout. Last March when the shop closed I became a TV presenter on the show Sewing Street for about six months. But I had to travel to Birmingham which was a five-hour trip and I wasn't happy with the COVID precautions so I stopped that. Then I spent months in my studio designing. My husband is a furniture designer and he hasn't had a day off since this started.

During lockdown I have seen a lot more people interested in knitting and maybe postbox toppers came partly from that and from having more time on people's hands. But I think there is also a lot of mindfulness involved in making something tangible and so detached from what is going on in your daily life. People can get a lot of joy from something beautiful that has taken work and care. That can be very rewarding a time like this."

FACT

More than **250,000 small businesses were at risk of collapse** without more government help, the Federation of Small Businesses warned in January 2021.

JULIA UNDERWOOD, 80,
Freelance copy-editor on using technology

"I was a scientist, I had a degree in physiology and I wanted to be a doctor but in the late 1950s they only took about 10% of women into teaching hospitals, so I started to work in research. But I got fed up living in London. I had broken up with my boyfriend, my job was going badly and I wanted to go abroad and have an adventure. My stepmother's brother was living in Jamaica so I asked if I could go and stay with him.

I taught myself to crochet when I was working at the British High Commission in Jamaica. I had a really boring job. My boss was never there so I spent my day crocheting, making mini dresses that were really fashionable then. I got really good at making them and started to sell them. This was in about 1968. We would get invited to cocktail parties onboard visiting ships and I remember one of the crew serving canapes trying to peer up my dress to see what I had on underneath as they were so short.

I met my husband when I got back to London and we got married. When our children were young I needed to have something I could do from home so I taught myself to make curtains and set up a curtain making business from that.

After living in France for six years we moved to Ruislip. My husband died in 2010. I have been here ever since. Over the years I have made many patchwork quilts, I do tapestry, clothes for Barbies dolls, but I am always searching for that perfect thing. I make things for lots of charities including Knit For Peace.

When lockdown hit it was not too bad for me. I have lived on my own for 10 years and always been quite self-sufficient. In a way I have quite liked lockdown because it takes away obligations. I have been very careful because I am in the age group that is most vulnerable and I have some lung issues. I wasn't told to shield. I did most of my shopping myself. I think I reacted fairly well except for getting chronic insomnia. I don't know why. When I wake up I either read or might play patience on the computer. I am not bad on technology and I am pretty dependent on the computer to stay in touch with people.

I have been amazed by the response to letterbox toppers. I really like them, some more than others. Everyone seems to be positive about them. They really have cheered people up. There are people who think we are being frivolous by putting things on top of letterboxes and I think that is mean spirited. You get those people who complain about Christmas lights on houses. But I don't think the toppers will go on forever. This has been the time for them. We needed something fun."

> **FACT**
> A study by live-in care agency Elder found one in five respondents aged over 70 spoke to family and friends less than every fortnight during the lockdown as **28% were not confident using technology**.

JULIA UNDERWOOD – **Ruislip, Hillingdon**

ALISON TUCKER, 63,

Self-employed, on surviving the loss of business

"I'd been making masks for charity and raised about £2,400 selling them in cafes in Bideford and Westward Ho (in Devon). It's been my therapy during lockdown to feel like I am doing something. Then I saw these toppers online and decided to have a go. They made me smile and I wanted to make others smile. I had a photo from the 1980s of my husband Andy with two of our three two sons on a beach and he was wearing socks with his sandals. It looked hilarious so I decided to make a beach scene with a man in socks and sandals, a seagull pinching chips and so on. I wanted to make it funny. I spent 12 days with 3 hours a day on it. My husband helped me make the deckchair from wood. I put it up anonymously but the response has been amazing and people love it.

My husband is self-employed with a few properties to manage and my three sons are all self-employed in the car industry. Two run a garage that my husband set up and the third has a workshop and a tuning lab. I've always been self-employed but I am semi-retired now. We used to run a care home but we closed it seven years ago as my husband has Parkinson's. We tried to sell it but we couldn't as it only had 15 beds so we closed it and we live there. We have let out part of it and we are renovating.

FACT

The Enterprise Research Centre said **22% of the self-employed, or 1.1 million people**, were in sectors most at risk of loss of livelihood in the COVID crisis.

We also run a holiday let in Spain near Alicante that we've had for 20 years. That has been tough as we've not had any help at all. We have only had one 10 day booking since lockdown started whereas we normally have at least six months booked. At the moment we are leaving it as it is and we're lucky we can afford to let it lie for a while. Being self-employed we got it so we could go when we wanted and the family could use it. At the start I tried to learn Spanish but I gave up. I'm too old now.

For people who are self-employed it has been tough during lockdown and a lot of businesses won't survive. It really was a shock for everyone and it has changed lives for sure. My sons were quiet workwise for a while, particularly on the MOT front, but it has picked up again now. I think people have changed their priorities because of COVID and it has made them think what they want to do with their lives.

I think the toppers are as wonderful as they are different. I don't think this would have happened without lockdown as people have more time on their hands. A lot of people have been speculating about who made mine and I like the anonymous bit. I've really enjoyed it as it makes me feel I'm making people smile during such a tough time."

ALISON TUCKER – **Westward Ho, Devon** PHOTO CREDIT

LORRAINE REED-WENMAN, 65,

Chair of the Middlesex Federation of Women's Institutes, on dealing with loneliness

"I have always been interested in crafts. I loved art at school. But when you start work you just don't have time for it. When I retired five years ago I decided to get into more crafts and I joined the WI because I didn't want to be stuck in front of the television.

I'm one of those people who can't just sit back. In a normal year I would run about 30 workshops on crafts for beginners. I thought during lockdown that I would be able to get on with all my unfinished projects but lockdown changes your life. I became three times busier than I was before. I run a Zoom session every Monday night called a craft-inn - yes, inn, as a few of us do like a glass of wine with our knitting and crochet. I've also been joining other meetings across the county as I can on Zoom. I've met more members than ever.

I thought everything was fine in the first three months of lockdown but then you realise that mental health problems are becoming a real issue. I just opened my doors. Crafting brings people together. It might take 2 or 3 sessions but then they might open up and start to talk to you, knowing you are not going to gossip.

We have lost four people over the past year which is four too many but age has a lot to do with things and underlying health conditions. You get some members who just won't be beaten by this but others are scared witless to go outside the front door, even with vaccinations. Other are still sanitizing everything that comes in the post.

I don't have children but I can talk to my husband. My father is 92 with dementia and 110 miles away on the coast. Throughout lockdown I have driven for six hours twice a week to see him. I get his shopping delivered to me then go from my drive to his drive. I doubt I could have got through this time without going to see him.

One of the good things that has happened in lockdown is that it has forced people to use iPads, Skype, smartphones, Zoom, FaceTime. I think what will happen is that the WI will have face-to-face meetings in future but also a Zoom link for people who are bit too frail or poorly or frightened to come out in the dark in winter. Technology will continue to play a big part because, let's face it, this thing is not going away.

When the postbox toppers started I just thought I had got to do that. I see people looking and stopping and it brings a smile to their faces. I think the coronavirus and lockdown made people rethink and re-evaluate their lives. People get so wrapped up with work, shopping, kids, and daily routines but lockdown forced people not to go out and gave people time to do something they enjoy. "

FACT

Age UK said it had never known a time when older people had needed its services so badly with about **one in three struggling** with loneliness and a feeling of alienation during the pandemic.

LORRAINE REED-WENMAN – **West Ruislip, Hillingdon**

MON

st Collection Time
onday to Friday
5.30pm

later collection is made at 6.30pm
from the Postbox at
Ruislip Delivery Office,
40 Parkway

Saturday
12 noon

Other Collections

Additional collections may be made throughout the day until
the last time shown.

03457 740740
www.royalmail.com
0345 6000606

NATHAN TRACEY, 17,

A-level student on applying for university

FACT

The number of applicants for university rose in 2020 to the **highest level in four years,** according to the Universities and Colleges Admission Service (UCAS)

"I don't knit or crochet but when my mum started making toppers we realised we could put a note up with them to raise money for charity. She asked me if I could make QR codes (Quick Response barcodes that can direct people to donation forms) and print them to put on the toppers. I googled it and worked out how to put them online. We did them for the London Ambulance, YoungMinds, and other charities. We tried to cover a fair range of charities. The QR codes went down quite well locally.

It wasn't that hard to do. I am doing computer science A-Level as well as maths and politics and I want to study computer science at university. It has been tough doing A-levels like this and would have been better not in lockdown. We probably missed about a third of the schooling. When lockdown first started for the first few months it really was just a case of working on your own but then it ramped up and we were getting online school. There was a gap but that was to be expected as schools were not prepared for this. There was a lot of uncertainty around it for us, particularly with exams and how you get grades. The unpredictability of it all has been hard. But I got an offer from Bath University and that is what I really wanted.

Lockdown did start to get very boring and a bit depressing. You wake up, walk two metres to your computer, do school, go back to bed. After months it started to grate a bit. You weren't seeing anyone for ages and it just went on and on. I was considering taking a gap year but you can't travel and it wouldn't be that much fun just being at home. I will go to university in September and hope there isn't another lockdown. With the vaccines, it does seem to be getting a bit better.

One thing during lockdown is that I have been able to put more time into my hobbies as there was not much else to do. I got into cycling more and I taught myself hacking. I really enjoy cyber security and you can do online challenges on websites like Hack the Box. They run ethical hacking challenges. I tried to teach myself that over lockdown. It is quite a big industry so it would be great to get into that. Someone will pay you to test sites for hackers. Scams have been a big thing during lockdown so this industry will just grow. I had texts that were meant to be from Royal Mail that were scams and one from HSBC and I don't even have an account with them.

I was glad I could help my mum with the QR codes. The toppers have really done so well over lockdown and been really appreciated locally."

NATHAN TRACEY - **Ruislip, Hillingdon**

MON

Last Collection Time

Monday to Friday

9.00am

A **4.00pm** or later collection is made
from the Postbox at
Evelyn Avenue,
Elmbridge Drive

The latest collection in the area is made
at **6.30pm** from
Pinner Post Office,
67 Bridge Road

Saturday

7.00am

LOUISE GREEN, 36,

Part-time receptionist on being furloughed

"I took up crochet when we went into lockdown. I work two days a week as a receptionist at my father-in-law's plumbing company but for the first 13 weeks of lockdown I was furloughed and stayed at home. I needed something to keep my mind occupied. My husband is a plumber in Sheffield so he was an essential worker but I was at home with our three children. We've got Lily who is 16, Dylan is 14 and Ruby is 12. When they were having their quiet time I found myself doing nothing so I decided to learn how to crochet. My grandma, who is 86 this year, has always crocheted. So has my aunt. It is something I had always wanted to do. Then I found out that I am really good at it.

For me it became a bit of an obsession. It gave me a reason to switch off what was happening everywhere in lockdown and everything we were seeing on the news. I started off making a few things, for babies, but then I saw the postbox toppers and I thought I would like to have a go. I didn't have a pattern but I worked it out. Mine is covered in flowers. Some of the toppers are really amazing. The amount of time and effort that goes into that is unbelievable!

I went back to work last June but crochet consumes you and I won't go back now to not crocheting. Lockdown has meant lots of different things to different people and crocheting was my saviour. Listening to the news was so upsetting that you needed something to stay focused on the fact that there would be a way out of this.

Seeing a smile on someone's face when they see your topper is wonderful. We live in an area that is not the best and you don't see things like this around here. I left a note with mine saying I hope this brings a smile to your face and called myself Crochet Lady as I didn't want my name out there. For my next one I am going to have a holiday theme – maybe a beach and a boat, that kind of thing - because a lot of people still aren't able to get away.

This time last year there was a lot of apprehension about what was going to happen and seeing a community pull together is great. I am a firm believer in giving back to the community and being kind and toppers have given everyone a reason to go for a walk and something to talk about. "

FACT

- -

As of March 15, 2021, about **11.4 million jobs, from 1.3 million different employers, were furloughed** in the United Kingdom as part of the government's job retention scheme.

LOUISE GREEN — **Sheffield** PHOTO CREDIT

JANE WOODLEY, 45,
Freelance video subtitler, on family life

"I learnt to crochet in 2014 when I was recovering from surgery for endometriosis. I thought I have to do something and not just watch Netflix. Since then I must have done millions of stitches. I taught myself with YouTube, a book, and a lot of swearing. In October 2019, I had a hysterectomy because I was fed up with severe endometriosis. In a way I was already very used to my world being smaller because of my medical history and having to stay in bed most months. I was good at occupying myself in the house and I have a good network of online friends through yarning.

When the local group in Eastcote and Ruislip started and everyone started coming out of the woodwork I was amazed. There was a handful of local things going on before that felt rather like we were on the 'Good Life' with Victoria sponges and home-grown marrows. But when this group started there were hundreds of people doing incredible things.

My oldest son, Fraser, was doing his GCSEs in 2020 so fairly early on he found out he was not going to have exams. He spent a lot of time cooking and baking bread. He is now training to be a chef. My middle son, James, has always worked at school but does not see home as a place for school work so he finds it hard to get motivated. He wants to follow in his brother's footsteps. My youngest George, who is obsessed by peacocks, has probably had to adjust the most. We are lucky that we all get along.

I have been doing a thing called Daily George when I started to take a photo of him every day as we went into lockdown as my parents and my mother-in-law weren't going to see him that much. He was premature, a month early, and very little when he was born so everyone feels very protective of him.

Family life has been OK for us. When lockdown first started and we didn't know what we coming it was all quite eerie, surreal. Normally you wake up from a nightmare but we all woke up in a nightmare. Now we are all lockdown veterans and talk about vaccinations and it is normal to take a mask everywhere.

Without a doubt though this has been a world changer. My business as a freelancer video subtitler has been busier than ever during this period and I have had moments of guilt and upped my charity donations and involvement so getting involved with toppers was ideal. They make you smile even if just internally. Anything you can do to make people smile when we have had so many moments of horror and fear must be good and they bring people together. It is a happy feeling to be part of something joyful, be it as the audience or the maker. It is like the yarn version of the Blitz Spirit."

FACT

- -

The Charities Aid Foundation found charity donation levels held up during the pandemic despite less in-person fundraising and sponsorship levels falling. Between January-June 2020, the public **donated £5.4 billion to charity, an increase of £800 million** on the same period in 2019.

JANE WOODLEY – **Eastcote, Middx**

SUE MOON, 60,

Marketing manager, on family in care homes

"When I saw something on Facebook about an arts and crafts group starting up near me and I thought I would join in and then someone came up with the idea of toppers. I had knitted in the past, so I knitted some flowers and I got the bug. You feel as if you are giving something back and being useful for once.

I have an immune disease and I have to take immuno suppressants so I was shielding. I was half expecting the letter telling me to shield but when it arrived we were a bit overwhelmed with terror initially. We all were. Those first few months were pretty grim. We were all washing the groceries at that point because we just didn't know what was coming.

We had put my father, who had dementia, in a care home twelve months earlier, so I couldn't see him. He didn't understand what was going on and why we couldn't visit him but I was shielding and the home in Wolverhampton had closed to visitors. I was finally able to see him in August and he passed away late August. It is a story that so many people can tell. You could only have 15 people to the funeral. He was 91 and he didn't die of COVID but I do think the isolation had something to do with it. For people like my father there was nothing for them to look forward to and I don't think they understood what was happening.

I run marketing for a financial boutique business advisory and investment company and normally I would work in Charing Cross, commuting into London three days a week. Now I am working four days a week from home. I am working

FACT

- -

By early 2021 **many care homes remained closed** to all but end-of-life visits in a bid to keep more infectious, rapid spreading strains of COVID-19 at bay

1,000 million percent more. My husband was working five days a week in Canary Wharf in London and is now working from home too. We just find there is no demarcation any more between work and home. We've got two grown-up children but they live elsewhere and are busy too. We are trying to force ourselves to leave the house every night at 6.30 to go for a walk. I just smile when people say it must be so much easier working from home. But will we ever go back to the office fulltime? I don't know. I think we have proved we can do this and that is a massive change for everybody.

The toppers have raised a smile and made a brightness in an otherwise dark period. There is a trail and maybe people are using it as a reason to go out. There has been a lot of benefits from them and I do hope they will continue even after this."

SAT

Last Collection Time
Monday to Friday
5.00pm

A later collection is made at **6.30pm**
from the Postbox at
Ruislip Delivery Office,
40 Parkway

Saturday
10.3

PRIORITY POSTBOX
SATURDAY
& SUNDAY

REBECCA CHANDRAMOHAN, 26,

Pharmacy assistant, on working in the NHS

"I did a bit of knitting when I was younger. My Nan taught me and my cousin. But I got back into it during lockdown as it really helped me to relax. My Mum also knits. I work for the NHS and I really have a full-on job. It's so nice to be able to come home and knit and relax. I made two corgis on a topper for the Queen's birthday that I was really proud of. I know knitting seems an odd hobby for someone young but I really enjoy it.

At the start of lockdown I was working in a community pharmacy in Boots and it was long hours. No one really knew how bad this was going to be and we weren't prepared for it. It was a total shock and so many people were frightened. We had to deal with that when people came in. I moved in December to work at a pharmacy in Watford General Hospital which is dealing with a lot of COVID cases. In January it was really stressful when a second wave hit. I was a bit worried, of course, about my health and taking COVID home to my parents but the hospital by then was really well prepared with PPE and we all got our vaccinations very quickly. We were well looked after. It has been so hard for hospital staff though as you really see the worst of it all.

You can see it is incredibly difficult for the nurses. They really do work so hard and it very stressful for them. The public response to nurses and frontline workers has been fantastic.

I was also out there joining Clap for Our Carers when it was held every Thursday. That support has meant a lot.

I really enjoy my job but this has been an exhausting year. I have been working in pharmacies for three years now after studying pharmaceutical science at university. During lockdown you need to find ways to wind down and relax which is where toppers came in for me. I am also glad that I continued to go to work as a lot of my friends who work in offices were just at home and that can be far worse and so lonely. No one I know has lost their job but quite a few have been furloughed. We haven't been able to see each other and it has been hard not to have that physical contact."

> **FACT**
> ------------------------------
> The number of people applying for nursing courses has risen by almost a third, or 32%, during the pandemic, according to statistics from the University Admissions Service.

REBECCA CHANDRAMOHAN – **Ickenham**

NATHAN SWAIN, 7,

Primary school pupil on how schools changed

"Toppers makes postboxes look more colourful and I really like them. When my mum said she was going to make one I thought she meant a knitted little postbox but when I realised I did think she was a bit potty. I wanted to help so we chose a book theme and I chose all things to put on the top from two of my favourite books when I was little, 'The Hungry Caterpillar' and 'The Tiger Who Came to Tea'. My favourite books now are Harry Potter. I have read the first three.

When Mum and Dad told me last year that I wasn't going to school I started crying. I had to stay at home and do home learning. We went on lots of walks but I really missed my friends. I did FaceTime once with my best friend Jonathan and once with George but it wasn't the same. Then in June my Mum and Dad, who are both teachers, went back to work and I went to school three days a week.

I was really glad to go back as I love school. There were only about 100 children in the school at first and we didn't have our class teacher but a teacher assistant. We didn't have to wear our uniforms and were allowed to go to school in our PE kit. We had to wash our hands a lot and sit at desks on our own and we weren't allowed to mix with the other years.

When I went into Year 2 in September most children were back and we were allowed to sit two at a desk but not in a group. We all face the front. At breakfast club and after-school club we can mix with all years but during schooltime we have to stick to just our year.

My friends all know I got involved making toppers and they think it is great. We put 'The Tiger Who Came to Tea' on a postbox near my school and my friends and I had to walk past it in the mornings. One time our homework was to walk around all of the different toppers locally. My favourites are the really colourful ones and the one I loved the best was on the book 'Aliens Love Underpants'. It had a flying saucer and lots of aliens and lots of pants. They make me laugh and I think people make them because they do make everyone smile."

FACT

Children with at least one parent or carer who was a critical worker were able to go to school or college if required by government rules but **parents and carers were advised to keep children at home if they could.**

NATHAN SWAIN – **Leverstock Green, Herts**

TINA THOMAS, 46,

A stay-at home mum on remote home schooling

"I've made toppers dating back to 2016. I saw some from Herne Bay in Kent where my family lives and decided to do one for Christmas. I am a cub scout leader and I thought it would be good for the children to post letters for Father Christmas in a special postbox. Our donations went up by about £300 that year. So the next year I did another and the next year another. When lockdown started I decided I would not only do Christmas ones. In total I've down about eight.

I am a stay-at-home mum with two boys, aged 14 and 10. Home schooling has been very, very difficult. The teenager wants to do the minimum possible. Also we are so rural that the schools cannot rely on us having internet connection. It was a case of self learning rather than remote learning for us and I feel my secondary school child has lost an entire year. Luckily I have a degree in engineering so I could help with maths but trying to teach your own children is a whole new thing. They take it differently from a teacher than from me.

We are surrounded by fields and open space but we have been really isolated as we live about five miles outside the village of Torphins in Aberdeenshire. My husband lives in England so from March to Christmas my boys and I were home together and we really didn't see anyone else. I tried to keep them busy. I made a teddy bear trail for some of the children locally so they could go on walks and have something to see. I did a fish hunt around another village. I took my children with me to help put them out to give them a walk with a purpose. Anything to keep positive. The boys are back at school now. They are both really sporty so it is great rugby has started again.

The toppers and trails gave me something to do. I tried not to look too far ahead. We were lucky in Scotland because we were a bit more relaxed than England regarding masks in schools and social distancing. I think Scotland will have a much better mental health outcome for the children.

The thing I found the hardest was not being able to see my dad for 18 months. He suffers from dementia and I am told now that he can't recognise his children anymore. For us in Scotland it doesn't make sense to go to Kent, a high-risk area.

I'll continue the toppers as there has been such positive feedback. I am going to take on another village. It is way to cheer up your community. I can't believe how many people are giving it a go – and the standard is getting better and better. Crafts are good for your own mental health as they keep you occupied when you are isolated."

> **FACT**
> ------------------------------------
> Almost two-thirds, or 63%, of home-schooling parents said in January 2021 that home-schooling was negatively affecting their children's well-being, compared with 43% in April 2020, according to the Office of National Statistics.

TINA THOMAS – **Torphins, Aberdeenshire** PHOTO CREDIT

PAULA HAMPSON, 50,

Pharmacy assistant, on mental health issues

"I live in a small village where I started a knit-and-natter group about six years ago. We decided it would be fun to yarn bomb the village so on gala day in 2017 we went all out and everyone loved it. We were asked to do it again. I did a postbox topper, a Rastafarian hat, but it was stolen. Then I spotted postbox toppers again online during lockdown and decided to make more. I am off work with mental health issues and making people smile is a nice thing to do when you don't feel smiley yourself.

I work in a community pharmacy and it was full on as soon as lockdown started. We were so worried about everything that my husband and I sent our daughter Evelyn, 8, to go and live with my parents. I didn't want to bring any nasties home. It was difficult as we were often working until 10 at night to keep up with the prescriptions. The doctors weren't seeing anyone at that time so pharmacies were swamped. Pharmacists really are unsung heroes. We kept our doors open through all of this.

My parents took Evelyn even though my mum had just come out of hospital after being treated for cancer. We didn't see Evelyn for three months apart from FaceTime. Evelyn did really well. I am so proud of her. She would settle down and do her homework.

When the second lockdown started I wasn't so worried and I was happier sending Evelyn to school as a key worker's child. The most kids in a classroom at any time was six. My parents both got COVID but I didn't. My mum had to go back to hospital with food poisoning earlier this year and she caught it there. She gave it to my dad. They are OK now.

By the time of the third lockdown things were really getting on top of me. There was so much going on at work and it ended up being too much. I stopped work in April on stress leave. I was having panic attacks. Of course this is related to COVID. It has been a very stressful time for everyone.

My first topper was in April when I stopped working. I've been crocheting since I was about 11 and crochet is my safe, happy place. My first one was for St George's Day then I did the Millennium Falcon from Star Wars for May the Fourth. Some people know it is me but not many. I think it is the quirky British sense of humour that has made them so popular. No one else has got postboxes like us really and we are all a bit daft and a bit eccentric. Lockdown has brought out the Dunkirk spirit in a lot of people."

> **FACT**
> ------------------------------------
> Over a fifth of people in Britain experienced some form of depression between January 27 and March 7, 2021, **more than double pre-pandemic figures,** with the impact felt more greatly in women, young adults, and those living alone, according to the Office for National Statistics.

PAULA HAMPSON – **Overseal, Derbyshire** PHOTO CREDIT

ANITA WARBURTON, 41,

NHS carer, on battling cancer

"When the first lockdown happened I was at home with my two children who are 10 and 12. I was home-schooling my son who is autistic and my daughter who has ADHD and everyone was really miserable. Then I spotted a rainbow theme with people putting rainbows in their windows for the NHS so I decided to crochet one for our high street. I got a hula hoop and cut it in half and made a giant rainbow for outside Sainsbury's. I was nervous because I had never left any form of crochet out before – I've been crocheting for about eight years - but everyone loved it. It was around that time I spotted a postbox topper on Facebook and that inspired me to do one for our post office. My first one was to commemorate the 75th anniversary of VE Day in May 2020.

I was working at Wexham Park Hospital near where I live in Farnham Common (Bucks) as an NHS ward host, cheering up the patients, when the pandemic started. Before that I was an environmental scientist but I was made redundant. At the hospital everyone was a bit stressed and anxious but trying their best. No one could come in to see their family members or friends and it was very frustrating and scary for some.

Then the tables turned in November when I found a lump in my breast. It turned out to be stage three breast cancer. I have no idea why as I never drank or smoke, just did crochet and watched TV. That is another reason why I am crocheting like crazy because it keeps me busy. I had a lumpectomy just before Christmas and had to have the lymph nodes in my left arm removed. I am having chemotherapy then radiotherapy and 10 years of chemotherapy tables. I was worried I wouldn't be able to crochet but actually it has helped keep my arm flexible.

This made me re-evaluate life. My hair has gone but that will grow back. Being diagnosed with cancer at this time meant I couldn't join any groups in person with others going through the same thing. I have joined Facebook groups and met one girl, Claire, who has the same diagnosis. We are very connected as we are on the same chemotherapy regime but one day apart and we both have dogs called Lulu. We call ourselves the Pink Sisters. She lives in Kent and we've never met but once our treatment is over we will definitely meet up for a drink.

It has been a hard year with lockdown and the diagnosis. I love doing toppers as it is so therapeutic. I have made about eight. They're fun and different and make people smile because you don't expect a postbox in a hat with things on top of it. This wouldn't have happened on this scale without lockdown but lockdown has made people want to cheer other people up."

FACT

The number of people being diagnosed with cancer early in England plummeted during the pandemic, with official data showing **a third fewer cancers detected at stage one** with normal NHS services disrupted, according to Public Health England and Macmillan Cancer Support.

ANITA WARBURTON - **Farnham Common, Bucks**

RACHEL WILLIAMSON, 58,

Retired police officer, on crime levels

"I've made over 70 toppers and I have a list as long as my arm to do still. At the start of lockdown I went to the chemist to get my mum's prescription and there was a queue with all these miserable faces so I decided to put a sparkly rainbow topper on a postbox nearby to cheer people up. It went bonkers. We were getting up at 6.30 am and going on our bikes to put them up. The local papers started asking who was doing them and found out through Facebook.

I retired nearly three years ago from the police after 18 years. I was a detective investigating child abuse. I was in uniform to start off with then a domestic abuse office and then I moved to child protection. I did that for 12 years until I was 55 and took the pension. I was 37 when I joined the police, married with three children and a manageress of a shop in the town centre. I applied to the police force three times when I was younger but I was told I didn't have what it takes. But I didn't

FACT

Crime levels dropped significantly at the start of the pandemic, specifically in theft and domestic burglary as everyone was at home. As lockdown measures were relaxed, crimes bounced back, according to the Office of National Statistics.

want to grow old not having tried again so I tried again. It was certainly my calling. I qualified as a detective and retired as a detective and I am quite satisfied with my lot.

The police did help me out. I made a seagull, Dave, for a topper and he got pinched, upsetting everyone. But the North Wales Police recovered him from an address in Rhyl while on another matter. I put him back on and someone pulled his head off. I had to redo that. More recently someone ripped an octopus off one of my toppers and threw it in the sea. The police phoned and said they had CCTV of someone and did I want to make a complaint. I said yes because hours go into these toppers. They let me know that the person responsible had mental health issues and has now left the area. The hotel where he was living made a £100 donation to help me buy wool for another.

It has been absolutely unbelievable since we started – and I say we, as my mum has knitted bits and my twin sister Ruth helped put them together. It's like being famous. I can't get out of my car in Rhyl without people stopping me. People have been buying the toppers, with some going to local museums. We did one for 'I Am a Celebrity' held at Gwrych Castle with Ant and Dec on it and the castle has asked for that one.

After 18 years in the police this has restored my faith in people. I realise there are some lovely people out there. We've had several pinched and several damaged but I've come to the conclusion that the good outweighs the bad. I just want to cheer people up and it has kept us positive."

RACHEL WILLIAMSON – **Rhyl, Wales** PHOTO CREDIT

05.
Lockdown Timeline

2020

16/04/20

Hemel Hempstead

March 26
First **Clap for Our Carers** tribute from doorsteps around the country

26/03/20

March 23
First lockdown starts in UK with people ordered to **"stay at home"**

23/03/20

April 16
Lockdown extended for **"at least"** three weeks

16/04/20

April 16
Captain Tom Moore completes 100 laps of his garden to raise money for the NHS

Ickenham

05/03/20

March 05
First death from coronavirus in the UK confirmed

Photo : Lynn Clegg, Wakefield

May 28
Tenth and final Clap for Our Carers staged

28/05/20

May 10
Conditional plan for **lifting lockdown**

10/05/20

Photo: Janice Welsh, South Shields

June 05
Number of recorded deaths passes **40,000,** according to the government

05/06/20

July 04
UK holds **a minute's silence** to remember those who died of COVID-19

04/07/20

Pinner

24/07/20

July 24
Face coverings become compulsory in shops & most other enclosed public places in England

06/06/20

June 06
BLM demonstrations held in cities across the UK

August 03
Eat Out to Help Out scheme begins in UK

16/08/20

September 01
Majority of schools in England, Wales and N. Ireland **reopen**

01/09/20

Photo: Abbey Thorne, Clacton-on-Sea

August 16
The shielding programme ends in Wales, the last part of the UK to do so

September 05
Six months after first death, a **total of 41,678** have died of COVID

05/09/20

October 02
Around a quarter of the UK population, **about 16.8 million people, are in local lockdowns**

02/10/20

14/10/20

October 14
The first COVID-19 tier regulations come into force with **three levels**

Ruislip

October 31
The UK reaches **one million** COVID-19 cases

31/10/20

Photo: Secret Society of Hertford Crafts

05/11/20

Photo : Sandra Luckett, Liverpool

November 05
Second **national lockdown** comes into force in England

Photo: Faversham Gunpowder WI

December 08
Margaret Keenan becomes the **1st person to get a COVID-19 vaccination**

07/11/20

Ickenham

November 07
Queen Elizabeth wears a face covering in public for the 1st time

02/12/20

December 02
Second lockdown ends with tier system in place

08/12/20

2021

31/01/21

02/02/21

February 02
Captain Sir Tom Moore died **aged 100**

Photo: Tunbridge Wells Yarnbomber

06/01/21

January 06
England enters **third national lockdown** and Scotland too

January 31
Figures show **8.98 million** people have received first COVID vaccination?

Ruislip

March 05
One year since the first COVID-19 death, number of deaths at **124,903** with 4.2 million cases

05/03/21

February 24
Number of people to receive first COVID vaccine hits **18 million**

24/02/21

29/03/21

March 29
Stay at home order for England comes to an end

Photo: Tricia Glenister, Hemel Hempstead

09/04/21

April 09
Prince Philip, Duke of Edinburgh, died **aged 99**

Ickenham

Photo Kathleen Shannon Great Dunmow

18/04/21

April 12
Outdoor **hospitality reopens** in England as well as shops, hairdressers, gyms

12/04/21

April 18
FA Cup semi-final held as a pilot event at Wembley Stadium

May 17
Pubs and restaurants allow customers indoors, up to **30 people** can meet outside

21/06/21

04/05/21

May 04
Care home residents are permitted to leave their residence for low-risk trips

17/05/21

June 21
Legal limits on social contact scheduled **to end**

Photo: Gemma Love, Beccles

06.
Lockdown Moments

From panic buying of toilet rolls to online exercise classes, here are 50 memorable moments, people and trends that emerged during lockdown in Britain.

1. Badgers started to appear on city streets including one filmed in a deserted concourse outside Sheffield Station; a herd of goats were seen in the empty streets of Llandudno, and other wildlife also emerged in droves.

2. Beards became a trend as barbers closed and men working from home gave up on shaving.

3. Bread making took off, particularly sour dough bread and banana bread.

4. Bikes: SOLD OUT.

5. Birdsong suddenly became noticeable as air and road traffic plummeted.

6. Black Lives Matter protests were held nationwide in the summer of 2020, described by British historians as the largest anti-racism rallies since the slavery era. The protests were inspired by the BLM movement in the United States and killing of George Floyd by a white police officer.

7. Boardgames were back in vogue as families stayed home, with top sellers including Connect 4, Monopoly and Codenames.

8. Book sales soared, with more than 200 million print books sold in the UK in 2020, the first time since 2012 that number had been exceeded, according to official book sales monitor Nielsen BookScan.

9. Bucket lists started to be drawn up as people dreamt of travel and adventures.

10. Captain Tom Moore, a retired British army officer, won the nation's hearts as he walked a hundred lengths of his garden in the run-up to his 100th birthday in April 2020 to raise money for the NHS. He became a household name, raised more than £30 million. He was knighted in July 2020 by the Queen. He died in February 2021.

11. Clap for Our Carers began on March 26, 2020, and ran for 10 weeks with millions of people across the UK taking to their doorsteps with pots and pans to applaud NHS staff and other key workers.

12. Householders decluttering their homes, and prompting charity shops - when open - to restrict how many contributions they would take.

13. Colour-coordinated bookshelves became a trend as people's reading habits could be seen behind them on video calls.

14. Coronials were set to replace millennials as the generation of babies conceived or born in lockdown.

15. Covidiot was coined as the name for people ignoring public health advice.

16. Dalgona coffee infiltrated Instagram feeds with pictures galore of this Korean frothy iced coffee made from instant coffee, sugar, and hot water whisked into a stiff peak and put on top of milk.

17. Dominic Cummings, chief adviser to Prime Minister Boris Johnson, outraged the nation after it was revealed that he travelled from London to County Durham after the start of lockdown to stay with his parents and sister. During the stay he visited local beauty spot, Barnard Castle, which he said was a drive to test his eyesight.

18. Doomscrolling, or the act of compulsively scrolling through social media or news feeds which relate to bad news, preoccupied so many people during 2020 that the Oxford English Dictionary named it a word of the year and added it to the dictionary.

19. Eat Out to Help Out schemes ran throughout August 2020 with pubs and restaurants offering 50% discounts up to the value of £10 a person which cost the government about £850 million to finance.

20. Fairy lights became a must-have in gardens.

21. Furlough became part of our daily language as the government stepped in to pay 80% of employees' wages when lockdown meant there was nothing for them to do at work.

22. Gardening became a national obsession with growing your own vegetables taking off.

23. Gazebos: SOLD OUT.

24. Handforth Parish Council in Cheshire hit the headlines when a Zoom video of a meeting descending into chaos went viral with councillors trading insults and several quotable moments. Stand-in clerk Jackie Weaver was told: "You have no authority here" – and she kicked out the chairman.

25. Joe Wicks, aka The Body Coach, a fitness instructor from Surrey, got the nation moving as he televised short workouts every morning, saying he wanted to be "the PE teacher for the nation".

26. Loungewear sales surged with online fashion giant Missguided reporting sales skyrocketing 700% in 2020 as people got comfy and turned to exercise in the new work from home culture.

27. Macne became a new word, meaning skin eruptions caused by face masks.

28. Marcus Rashford, the Manchester United footballer, became a household name after campaigning to extend the free school meal scheme for children into the summer holidays. He raised £20 million for the charity FareShare that distributes food to vulnerable children.

29. Margaret Keenan, from Coventry, was the first woman in Britain – and the world – to receive a COVID-19 vaccination. Aged 90 at the time, she said it was the "best early birthday present" she could wish for as she could finally spend time with her family and friends.

30. "Normal People" catapulted Paul Mescal and Daisy Edgar-Jones into fame as the most watched BBC series in 2020.

31. Patio heaters: SOLD OUT.

32. PPE or Personal Protective Equipment became part of everyday conversations.

33. Puppies were in such demand that prices soared – as did dog thefts with a reported 19% increase in 2020. Benchmark Kennels found the average asking price for puppies ranged from £1,050 to £3,700 in 2021, over double pre-lockdown 2020 prices.

34. Roblox, a game creation platform with more than 50 million games and brightly coloured Lego-like avatars, took off as the most popular online entertainment forum for children aged seven to 13.

35. Quarantinis replaced office drinks in the pub at the end of the week with drinks online instead.

36. "Queen's Gambit" was the most watched TV show on Netflix in 2020, prompting a rush on chessboards.

37. Quizzes were organised among friends, families, and colleagues, with varying degrees of popularity.

38. Staycations surged as people took their holidays in the UK rather than in far-flung destinations.

39. TikTok, the video sharing app, became an obsession with even Dame Judi Dench and her grandson doing a dance video.

40. "Tiger King" was the first Netflix show to go viral during lockdown in April 2020.

41. Toilet rolls, pasta, flour, and yeast disappeared off shop shelves in panic buying.

42. Two metres social distance became the norm with the gap marked with stickers on pavements and on shop floors.

43. Vaccines became part of daily discussions as people compared dates of their vaccinations, the types from Pfizer to the AstraZeneca/Oxford to Moderna, and how they felt after the jab.

44. Volunteers appeared in their millions across the country to help in any way they could, with more than 750,000 signing up to a phone app to help the NHS which had set out to get 250,000 volunteers.

45. Walking became the main form of exercise for millions of people around the country.

46. WFH as an abbreviation for Working From Home no longer needed to be spelt out.

47. Wild swimming had already become popular but went crazy as swimming pools closed and more people raved about the health benefits of a cold dip.

48. Yoga with Adriene on YouTube, run by the American yoga teacher Adriene Mishler, inspired a new band of yoga enthusiasts.

49. "You're on mute" became one of the most used terms of lockdown, while "unmute" was named by Oxford Languages, publisher of the Oxford English Dictionary, as one of its words of 2020.

50. Zoom surged in popularity to have about 300 million daily meeting participants compared to 10 million in December 2019 – a 2900% jump.

07.
Lockdown Letterbox Locations

A

Alfreton, Derbyshire

B

Barnehurst, SE London
Barnham, West Sussex
Barnoldswick, Lancashire
Barrow, Suffolk
Belper, Derbyshire
Birchington-on-Sea, Kent
Birmingham, W. Midlands
Budleigh, Devon
Bushey, Herts

C

Caerleon, Wales
Canvey-on-Sea, Essex
Chesterfield, Derbyshire
Chippenham, Wiltshire
Church Stretton, Shropshire
Clacton-on-Sea, Essex
Cullompton, Devon

D

Didsbury, Manchester
Dundee, Scotland

E

Eastcote, Middx
Edinburgh, Scotland

F

Farnham Common, Bucks
Faversham, Kent
Felixstowe, Suffolk
Fenton, Staffordshire
Filey, Yorkshire
Finstall, Worcestershire
Frimley Green, Surrey

G

Gilberdyke, Yorkshire
Gorleston-on-Sea, Norfolk
Great Totham, Essex
Great Dunmow, Essex
Grays, Essex

H

Hampton, Richmond
Harefield, Hillingdon
Harwich Quay, Essex
Havering-atte-Bower, Greater London
Heather, Leicestershire
Hebburn, Tyne & Wear
Hertford, Herts
Hemel Hempstead, Herts
Histon & Impington, Cambridgeshire
Hoo, Kent
Hopton, Norfolk
Hornchurch, E. London
Horwich, Bolton, Greater Manchester
Hutton, Essex

I

Ickenham, Hillingdon
Isleworth, Hounslow

K

Kenilworth, Warwickshire

L

Leeds, Yorkshire
Leicester, Leicestershire
Leigh-on-Sea, Essex
Lincoln, Lincolnshire
Liverpool, Merseyside
Llandudno, Wales
Lowestoft, Suffolk

M

Manchester, Greater Manchester
Melton Mowbray, East Midlands
Moorthorpe, Yorkshire

N

Netherfield, Nottinghamshire
Northfleet, Kent
Nottingham, Nottinghamshire

P

Pinner, Middx
Portsmouth, Hampshire
Prestatyn, North Wales

R

Reading, Berks
Rhyl, Wales
Ruislip, Hillingdon

S

Saddleworth, Greater Manchester
Salford, Greater Manchester
Salisbury, Wiltshire
Scunthorpe, Lincolnshire
Sheffield, Yorkshire
Sheldon, Devon
Snainton, Yorkshire
Sneyd Green, Stoke-on-Trent, Staffordshire
Springfield, Wigan, Lancashire
Southend-on-Sea, Essex
Southwold, Suffolk
St. Albans, Herts
Stapleford, Nottinghamshire
Stevenage, Herts
Syston, Leicestershire
Sunderland, Tyne & Wear
Swadlincote, Derbyshire

T

Tarporley, Cheshire
Torphins, Aberdeenshire, Scotland
Tunbridge Wells, Kent

U

Upton, Dorset

W

Wakefield, Yorkshire
Watergate, Sleaford, Lincolnshire
West Bromwich, W. Midlands
Westward Ho, Devon
Whitton, Richmond
Winsford, Cheshire
Winton, Dorset
Witchford, Cambridgeshire
Woodley, Reading, Berks
Wrexham, North Wales

08.
Acknowledgements

We would like to thank all the family and friends who have supported us on this unique journey, some of whom thought it was a bit weird but most appreciated our desire to highlight something positive that came out of such a tough period. Belinda would particularly like to thank her long-suffering husband Rick who could not escape her daily brainstorming on their morning walks with their dogs Ozy and Luna even if he tried.

We also want to thank all of the knitters and crocheters across Britain who gave us their time, their stories, and shared their wonderful toppers with us as we researched Lockdown Letterboxes. The amount of work and love that went into every single one was remarkable. Without fail, positivity radiated from everyone we spoke to as they selflessly helped to cheer up their communities, often raising money for charity in the process. We also want to thank the Royal Mail for turning a blind eye to these unofficial works of street art.

But most important, we would like to thank all of the key workers around the country who worked so hard to keep us safe and well during this extraordinary time. From NHS staff, to teachers, postal workers, delivery drivers, local shopkeepers, supermarket staff, refuse collectors, cleaners, and transport workers, we applaud you.

Belinda, Rose, Pia and Keren

Printed in Great Britain
by Amazon

43133116R00048